Ben and Jerry

Other titles in the Inventors and Creators series include:

Alexander Graham Bell
Milton Bradley
Roald Dahl
Walt Disney
Thomas Edison
Albert Einstein
Henry Ford
Benjamin Franklin
Jim Henson
Jonas Salk
Dr. Seuss
Steven Spielberg
The Wright Brothers

Ben and Jerry

P. M. Boekhoff

KIDHAVEN PRESS

An imprint of Thomson Gale, a part of The Thomson Corporation

THOMSON

GALE

Detroit • New York • San Francisco • San Diego • New Haven, Conn. • Waterville, Maine • London • Munich

For more information, contact
KidHaven Press
27500 Drake Rd.
Farmington Hills, MI 48331-3535
Or you can visit our Internet site at http://www.gale.com

LIBRARY OF CONGRESS CATALOGING-IN-PUBLICATION DATA

Boekhoff, P. M. (Patti Marlene), 1957–
Ben and Jerry / by P.M. Boekhoff.
   p. cm. — (Inventors and creators)
Includes bibliographical references.
Summary: Discusses the lives of Ben Cohen and Jerry Greenfield, creators of Ben & Jerry's Ice Cream.
ISBN 0-7377-2611-3 (hardback: alk. paper)
   1. Ben & Jerry's (Firm)—History—Juvenile literature. 2. Cohen, Ben (Ben R.)—Juvenile literature. 3. Greenfield, Jerry—Juvenile literature. 4. Businesspeople—United States—Biography—Juvenile literature. 5. Ice cream industry—United States—History—Juvenile literature. I. Title. II. Series.
   HD9281.U54B462 2004
   338.7'6374'0922—dc22
2004007901

Printed in the United States of America

Contents

Chapter One

Two Kids from Long Island

Millions of people enjoy Ben & Jerry's ice cream every day, and it is one of the most popular brands of ice cream in the United States. But the men behind the ice cream, Bennett Cohen and Jerry Greenfield, did not plan to become rich and famous by selling ice cream. It was only through years of hard work and dedication to their business that Ben and Jerry achieved great success.

Ben and Jerry did not know each other as young children, but they had a lot in common. They were both born in Brooklyn, New York, in 1951. They grew up fewer than two miles (3.2 kilometers) away from each other in Merrick, Long Island, a short train ride away from New York City.

Most of all Ben and Jerry both loved food. When Ben was young he mashed up his favorite cookies and candies into his ice cream after dinner. Ben learned from his dad, who could eat an entire half gallon of ice cream out of the carton after dinner.

Ben and Jerry were both overweight, and other kids made fun of them. Jerry was called Fatty, and Ben sometimes split his pants when he bent over on the playground. Jerry tried to fit in, playing sports with the other children in the school yard. But Ben did not like playing sports. Instead he and a friend started a Clean Plate Club for kids who finished all their lunch.

Ben and Jerry were both very smart kids, but Ben did not like to study. Still, without even trying, Ben got the best marks in his sixth-grade class. He performed brilliantly on intelligence tests and was voted most likely to succeed. Jerry paid attention in class and remembered

Ben and Jerry were both born in Brooklyn, New York (pictured), in 1951.

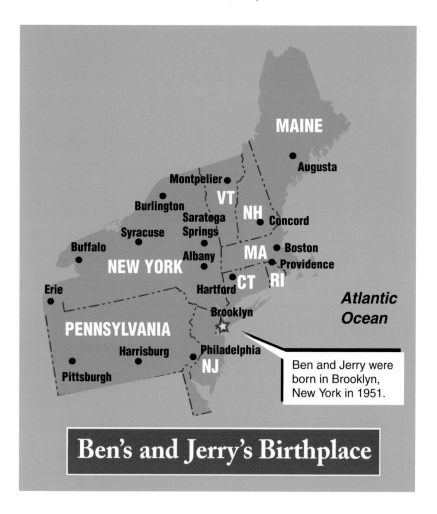

Ben and Jerry were born in Brooklyn, New York in 1951.

Ben's and Jerry's Birthplace

what he was taught. He worked on his homework and got very good grades.

First Meeting

In 1963 Ben and Jerry met at Merrick Junior High School, where they were both in advanced classes. They were still overweight, so they were the slowest kids in the seventh-grade gym class. One day the coach yelled at them while they were running far behind all the other kids on the track. He said that if they could not run around the track in fewer than seven minutes, they would have to do it again.

Ben questioned the logic of the rule. He asked, "But coach, if we can't do it in less than seven minutes the first time, how are we gonna do it in under seven minutes the second time?"[1] Ben sometimes protested against rules he thought were unfair. Jerry liked that about Ben. At that moment Jerry saw Ben as someone he could be friends with. The friendship was interrupted, however. In the eighth grade Ben was transferred to a different junior high school.

High School Friends

In the fall of 1966, Ben and Jerry were reunited when both went to Calhoun High School. The two became

Ben Cohen (left) and Jerry Greenfield became friends in seventh grade and graduated from the same high school in 1969.

close friends, spending time together after school and sometimes going on double dates in Ben's convertible.

Ben was a creative rebel who did only what he wanted to do. He played the cello, edited the school yearbook, was on the student council, and was good at **debate**. But he was not interested in classes. He read what he wanted and not what the teachers assigned.

Unlike his friend, Jerry obeyed his teachers and was at the top of his class. He was very smart and thought of himself as a nerd. He worked hard at his homework, and his grades were third best out of six hundred kids.

College Boys

When Ben and Jerry graduated in 1969, they both decided to go to college. Jerry was interested in medical science. Ben was interested in art, but his dad tried to talk him out of studying in that field. Ben's father did not think an artist could make a good living.

Ben's dad helped him apply to Colgate University in New York. Ben agreed to go. But Ben was not interested in what the professors were trying to teach him, and he did what he wanted. As a result he got bad grades.

Jerry went to Oberlin College in Ohio to study **premed**, which means he took classes that would help him get into medical school. Although Jerry wanted to attend medical school, he was not completely serious about wanting to be a doctor. Jerry fit in at Oberlin and did well.

Ben went to Colgate University (pictured), but dropped out in his second year because he was not interested in what the professors were teaching.

Drifting Back Together

In their second year of school Ben dropped out of Colgate and visited Jerry at Oberlin. Jerry had just finished his favorite class, Carnival Techniques, in which he learned tricks performed by circus entertainers. In the class Jerry learned to swallow fire and smash a **cinder block** on someone's belly without causing harm. Using this newfound knowledge, Ben and Jerry put on a circuslike show on campus. Ben acted the part of Habeeni Ben Coheeni, mystic madman. He wrapped himself up in sheets, and Jerry smashed a cinder block on his belly.

Ben and Jerry lived together in Greenwich Village for a year after Jerry graduated from Oberlin College. Pictured is Washington Square, a park in Greenwich Village.

After his visit Ben was restless. He drifted from place to place and from job to job. He hitchhiked back to Merrick and got a job loading ice cream onto trucks. He studied art at Skidmore College in Saratoga Springs, New York, for a year. Then he moved to Greenwich Village, an arty neighborhood in New York City. He had lots of different kinds of jobs, but none lasted more than a few months.

Meanwhile, Jerry stayed in school and studied medical science. He got involved in sports and got into shape. He was a good student but not good enough to be accepted into medical school. In May 1973 he graduated from Oberlin and moved into Ben's apartment in New York. He took **biochemistry** classes and got a job doing research in a laboratory.

A Discovery

Jerry worked during the day, and Ben worked at night. When Jerry came home he found chunks of burned toast scattered around the apartment. Jerry soon learned that his roommate did not have a very good sense of smell or taste. He found that Ben could not taste bland food. Ben often did not finish eating food such as bread and butter, and so he set it down and forgot about it.

Jerry also found out that Ben could not smell the toast burning, or feel the bread in his mouth if it was too soft. Ben could only taste food if it had an intense flavor. He could only feel it in his mouth if it had a crunchy texture, such as the ice cream with cookies and candy he made as a child.

Business Moves

In the fall of 1974 Ben found a job in which he could combine his interests in food and art. He moved to the country and got a job at a school. There he was an art teacher and cook for children who were addicted to drugs and mentally disturbed. Among his many projects, he and the children wrote and filmed a play about a school where everyone became addicted to chocolate milk powder. The film was a favorite at the school.

Meanwhile, Jerry fell in love with Elizabeth Skarie, a nursing student who soon became his girlfriend. Elizabeth got a job in North Carolina, and she and Jerry moved there together in 1974. Jerry found a laboratory job and continued his studies, but he still could not get into medical school.

By January 1977 Elizabeth had broken up with Jerry, and Ben's job ended when the school where he worked was closed. Ben tried to sell some pottery he made. But when he realized he could not support himself that way, he decided to talk to Jerry about starting a business together.

Chapter Two

The Ice Cream Shop

In May 1977 Jerry loaded up his car and moved back to New York. He and Jerry decided to start a business. "We were clearly not succeeding in our chosen fields," Jerry said. "So we started considering different ways to support ourselves. Since we love to eat, we immediately thought of food."[2]

Ben loved ice cream, so they decided to open an ice cream shop in a small college town. To research their new project they visited homemade ice cream shops. To learn the business they decided to take an ice cream–making class by mail, splitting the five-dollar cost of the course. After traveling to several college towns, they decided to open their shop in Saratoga Springs, where Ben had studied art at Skidmore College.

Drifting Along

Ben and Jerry moved to Saratoga Springs and found an apartment on the shores of Saratoga Lake. Saratoga Springs had a college, many summer tourists, and no ice cream shop. They decided they would each invest four thousand dollars in their new business.

Jerry had some money saved, but Ben needed to earn more to meet his half, so he worked in restaurants. While Ben worked as a cook, Jerry looked for a place to open their business. On the weekends they traveled to auctions to find used restaurant equipment for their business.

When they realized they were not doing well in their chosen fields, Ben (left) and Jerry decided to open an ice cream shop in a small college town.

Sometimes they were distracted, however. At one garage sale they bought a sailboat and trailer because it was a bargain at only two thousand dollars. This was despite the fact that Ben was not even close to having his share of money for the business.

Ben read the instruction manual for the sailboat out loud as they learned to sail. The summer was fun, and their business idea was slowly moving forward. Then in August someone else opened a homemade ice cream shop in Saratoga Springs.

The Work Begins

Ben and Jerry decided quickly to move to another college town without an ice cream parlor. They chose Burlington, Vermont. In late September they settled in and started looking for a place for their ice cream shop.

In October and November they made up a business plan and tried to get a bank loan. The bank loaned them four thousand dollars. Ben's father, happy that his son wanted to be a businessman instead of an artist, paid half of Ben's four thousand.

On December 17, 1977, Ben and Jerry's Homemade Inc. became an official business. Ben got to have his name first because it sounded better. Jerry got to be president because Ben got to have his name first.

In February they rented part of a leaky, unheated, old gas station that had four inches of ice on the floor. The ceiling was covered with soggy insulation and sagging plastic. In order to fix up their new store, Ben and Jerry worked day and night using the cheapest possible materials.

In 1978 Ben and Jerry opened their first ice cream shop in an old gas station in Burlington, Vermont (pictured).

Their friends helped them with the carpentry and plumbing in exchange for free ice cream for life.

Investing in Richness

Even though repairs on their new store took most of their money, Ben and Jerry chose only the highest quality ingredients for their ice cream. Jerry experimented with different recipes, using his knowledge of laboratory chemistry. He also asked Ben to taste the ice cream in order to figure out the formula for making the best flavors possible.

Jerry kept adding flavor until Ben could tell exactly what the flavor was, even with his very limited sense of taste. Jerry's ice cream contained almost twice as much flavoring as most ice cream. Jerry liked small chunks of fruit and candy in his ice cream, but he added lots of large chunks instead so Ben could feel them in his mouth.

To work out their ice cream flavors, Ben and Jerry used an old, unreliable, worn-out ice cream–making machine. Usually the ice cream was rich and creamy, but sometimes it was rubbery. Ben and Jerry ate it all. The only other food they spent money on was salty, white crackers and the cheapest canned fish. They invested everything they could to make the richest ice cream possible.

Despite having very little money, Ben and Jerry used only the highest-quality ingredients to make their ice cream.

A Busy Business

Ben and Jerry and their friends worked hard to get everything ready for their ice cream shop to open in spring. On opening day, May 5, 1978, the gas station was busy with activity and still under construction. Ben wanted the walls a slightly different color, so the painters repainted as the carpenters hammered. Jerry made ice cream. Ben made brownies, crepes, and soup while their friends helped serve people at the counter.

Every day people lined up to buy the rich-tasting, inexpensive ice cream. On their ninth day in business Ben

Instead of using regular advertising, Ben and Jerry decided to create fun, entertaining community events like building the world's largest ice cream sundae, which weighed nine tons.

and Jerry ran out of ice cream, and they kept running out until they could afford a new piece of equipment in June. After that they offered up to twelve flavors a day, and Jerry experimented with using homegrown fruit from local farmers and gardeners.

Ben and Jerry usually worked every day, about one hundred hours a week. Instead of stopping for lunch they scooped up customer leftovers and gulped them down in back of the store. Ben remembered, "The business was running us. We weren't running the business."[3]

Homemade Style

Although Ben and Jerry worked hard, they did not have money to advertise in newspapers or on television. Instead they had to find creative ways to promote their business. To promote their ice cream with eye-catching designs, Ben worked with graphic designer Lyn Severence to make art for their T-shirts, signs, and flyers.

To sell ice cream when the weather was cold, they organized community events. For example, in the fall they organized the Fall Down Festival with other businesses in the community. People dressed as ice cream ingredients and fell down together to look like an ice cream sundae. This event attracted large crowds who scooped up free ice cream samples provided by Ben and Jerry.

The Fall Down Festival also featured contests, such as frog jumping and ice cream eating. Elizabeth, Jerry's former girlfriend, came back and helped Jerry catch frogs from a nearby swamp for the frog-jumping contest. For entertainment Ben and Jerry brought back their old circus act from college. Jerry performed as Dr. Inferno, a fire-eater. He also smashed a concrete block on Habeeni Ben Coheeni's belly.

When the weather was warmer in spring and summer, Ben and Jerry attracted crowds in other creative ways. They projected free movies on the big building next door and invited people to come and watch. Sales were very good the first year, and Ben and Jerry put all the money they made back into connecting with their customers.

Instead of advertising, they entertained their customers with festivals, parties, movies, and circus acts. They made their ice cream part of the fun, giving it away to attract new customers with a free taste. They made their business different by having fun with their customers, co-operating with other businesses, and making their business an interesting and entertaining part of their community.

Chapter Three

The Ice Cream Factory

By the end of 1978 Ben and Jerry had created a one-of-a-kind ice cream business in Burlington, Vermont. They were well known in the town and had many loyal customers in the warm summer months. But they could not convince many people to come into their ice cream shop in winter. They tried to attract crowds by serving warm food such as soups and crepes, but these dishes were not very popular. There were plenty of leftovers, and Ben and Jerry ate most of them.

Ben's cooking was not very popular. But some restaurant owners wanted to sell Ben and Jerry's superrich ice cream, because ice cream was very popular in restaurants, even in winter. In January 1979 Ben decided to quit making crepes and start delivering ice cream in his old station wagon. He built an insulated box, filled it with big tubs of ice cream, and drove around Vermont delivering it to restaurants.

With demand increasing, Ben and Jerry realized that they could not possibly produce enough ice cream for the restaurants and their own shop that summer. To solve this problem they borrowed some money to set up a small ice cream factory in a big brick building. They bought an old ice cream delivery truck and had Lyn paint the side with a picture of big hands holding ice cream cones. On May 5, 1979, they had a one-year birthday party to celebrate the growth of their business and gave free ice cream to everyone who came to the party.

Jerry worked at the factory while Ben started up four summer ice cream stands. But even though they were making a lot of ice cream, they were still not making much money. One day Ben had a brilliant idea. Ben and Jerry would put their ice cream into pint containers. Ben could then sell them to grocery stores he passed on the road while delivering ice cream to the restaurants. Their ice cream would be sold as superpremium pints, the richest, most expensive kind on the market.

Ice Cream Fight

Jerry did not like Ben's idea at first because putting ice cream in pints would mean a lot more work for him at the factory. But in the end they agreed and spent a lot of money on containers with their pictures on the lid. Their pints were more expensive than most other superpremiums. So to attract customers they decided to use unusual ingredients such as chunks of cookie dough and pieces of candy bars, fudge brownies, apple pie, English toffee, and even cheesecake.

There were problems with the new idea, however. Jerry was using old machines to fill the small containers,

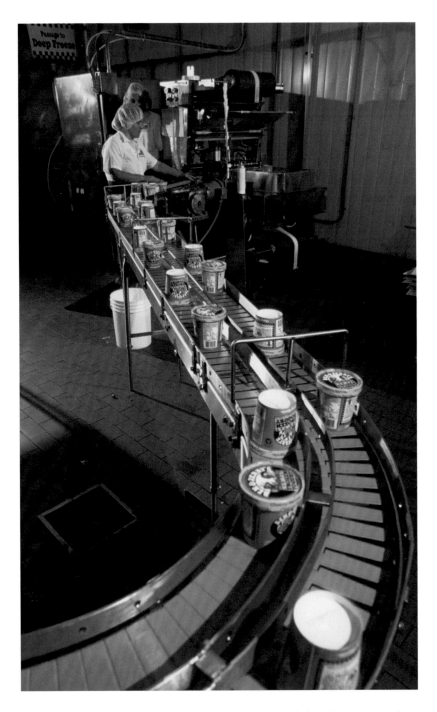

A conveyor belt at the Ben & Jerry's factory takes ice cream to the freezer.

A worker on the production line at Ben & Jerry's factory scoops chunks of cookie dough that will be mixed in with ice cream.

and the giant chunks were clogging it up. He often had to stick his hand in the cold ice cream to remove the chunks of food. Jerry told Ben he thought the chunks should be smaller so there would be a chunk in every bite, but Ben disagreed.

One day when Ben was helping Jerry at the factory, the argument turned into a fight. Every pint was filling only half full because of the big chunks, and Jerry had to fill the other half by hand. Ben was upset because his old truck was always breaking down. In the end they solved their problems by having the holes made larger in the filling machine and hiring **distributors** to deliver their ice cream.

Jerry Takes a Break

In April 1981 Ben and Jerry moved into a much larger factory, where they could make more ice cream. But Jerry was really tired from working sixteen hours a day, seven days a week, for three years. He was sixty pounds (27 kilograms) overweight from gulping down ice cream and fast food while working nonstop. Jerry needed a break. At the end of 1981 he decided to move to Arizona with his girlfriend, Elizabeth.

Ben talked his friend Fred "Chico" Lager into becoming a partner in the business. Together they added more freezers to the new, larger factory, and by 1983 their ice cream business doubled.

Growing Big

Even as Ben & Jerry's ice cream grew more successful, Ben refused to follow traditional business practices.

For example, when he visited important food delivery companies in Boston, he did not wear a suit and tie like most businessmen. Instead he tied his long hair back into a ponytail and came to meetings wearing ripped blue jeans. He gave away ice cream samples at meetings, letting the product do the talking.

Ben also used his creativity to build a bigger demand for Ben & Jerry's ice cream in Boston. He put up hundreds of posters announcing that two Vermont **hippies** were invading Boston with their ice cream. As part of the campaign Ben parked company ice cream trucks in front of office buildings. When workers came out into the streets on their lunch breaks, they were offered free Ben & Jerry's ice cream.

A Threat to Ben & Jerry's Ice Cream

While giving away ice cream to large crowds was fun, Ben had to face some serious business decisions. As the ice cream business kept growing Ben and Chico realized they would have to raise $3.5 million to build a big factory right away. But in March 1984, when he could not get a bank to give him a loan, Ben found out that his success was attracting unwanted attention. A powerful **corporation** that sold ice cream was trying to put Ben & Jerry's out of business. The corporation was threatening to take its business away from companies that delivered Ben & Jerry's ice cream to grocery stores. When the banks discovered this, they refused to loan Ben the money he needed.

Ben responded to the threat in his usual creative manner. He called Jerry, who was living in Arizona, and

When Jerry took a break from the business in 1981, Ben talked his friend Chico Lager (pictured) into becoming a partner in Ben & Jerry's.

In only six years, Ben & Jerry's Ice Cream grew from a small store in a former gas station to a major producer of superpremium ice cream with stores from Burlington, Vermont, to San Francisco.

asked him to protest outside the competitor's corporate building. Then he called reporters and told them Ben & Jerry's was being bullied by a gigantic corporation. The stories appeared as news all over the country with photos of Jerry protesting.

Ben rallied his loyal customers to protest and took out ads in the rock music magazine *Rolling Stone* that made fun of the giant corporation. Ben went directly to his customers for help. He printed a telephone number on the side of Ben & Jerry's ice cream cartons where people could leave messages of protest. He also ordered T-shirts and stickers to support the cause. And in the end, with help from their devoted customers, Ben and Jerry were able to stop the bullying tactics of the large corporation.

Ben and Jerry won their battle on Independence Day, the Fourth of July. In only six years they had turned a small business into a major producer of super-premium ice cream. With a little money and a lot of creativity, there seemed to be few limits on what these two old junior high school friends could accomplish.

Chapter Four

Giving Back

By 1985 Jerry had moved back to Vermont, and Ben and Jerry were working together again in the ice cream business. Their business continued to grow, and the two men continued to use their creative talents to do business in a new way. For example they bought a car that looked like a giant cow. In 1986 they traveled across America in the Cowmobile dishing up free ice cream to thousands of people. To further increase sales of their products they wrote *Ben & Jerry's Homemade Ice Cream and Dessert Book*, which contains ninety recipes for ice cream dishes to make at home.

By 1987 the company had hundreds of employees, which gave Ben and Jerry more time for their personal lives. Jerry married Elizabeth, who had become a psychologist. Their son Tyrone was born in late 1988. Ben married his girlfriend, Cindy, also a psychologist, and they had a daughter, Aretha.

Having children made Ben and Jerry think more about the future. They decided that they wanted to use more of their profits to make the world a better place. They had already set up a foundation that would give away almost eight out of every one hundred dollars they earned to social and environmental causes.

Ben and Jerry wanted to contribute more than just money to their favorite causes, however. They also wanted to donate their time. So they organized rallies and protest marches to promote environmental **conservation**, solar and wind energy, equal rights, peace, democracy, and the protection of children. These drew thousands of people who support these causes. In order

By the late 1980s, their company had hundreds of employees, and Jerry Greenfield (with wife and son) and Ben Cohen (with wife) finally had time to relax with their families.

Ben and Jerry have always donated their time and money to social and environmental causes. They are pictured here with a television monitor that shows an antiwar commercial they made in 2003.

to convince businesses to help improve the community, the men helped found Businesses for Social Responsibility, a network of more than fourteen hundred organizations. And, whatever the cause, Ben and Jerry gave away thousands of gallons of free ice cream at all their events.

Cherry Garcia

The social and environmental work supported by Ben and Jerry caught the attention of Jane Williamson and Marc Posner, who had a suggestion for the company. Williamson and Posner were Deadheads—fans of the band the Grateful Dead. They sent a postcard to Ben & Jerry's suggesting the company name an ice cream flavor after the Grateful Dead, writing: "You know it will sell . . . because Dead [related items such as T-shirts and stickers] *always* sell. We are talking good business sense here, plus it will be a real hoot for the fans."[4]

Ben and Jerry thought this was a very good suggestion. Both men liked the Grateful Dead's music. More important, the band remained dedicated to values that Ben and Jerry supported, such as peace and equal rights. Following through on this suggestion, Ben decided to make an ice cream with fudge flakes and cherries. And he gave it a clever name, Cherry Garcia, after the beloved Grateful Dead guitar player Jerry Garcia.

Cherry Garcia was the first ice cream ever named after a rock star. In February 1987, to celebrate this unique event, Ben & Jerry's took out an ad in *Rolling Stone* magazine promoting the ice cream. Cherry Garcia

Jerry Garcia was the first rock star to have an ice cream named after him.

was an instant hit with Deadheads—and thousands of people who simply liked the unique flavor. Within months it was among the company's three best-selling flavors.

Rainforest Crunch

The Grateful Dead continued to play an inspiring role for Ben and Jerry. In 1989 the group played a benefit concert to help save the rain forests in South America. Afterward, Ben decided to do something to help save the rain forest. He created a new flavor of ice cream, Rainforest Crunch, that used nuts grown by native people in the rain forest. By purchasing these nuts Ben

& Jerry's could support small farmers and help preserve the rain forest.

Ben had other benefits in mind as well. At the time, saving the rain forest was a popular cause. If customers associated ice cream with this worthy goal, they might buy more of the company's products. The project did not work out as planned, however. The ice cream flavor was very popular, and the company needed far more nuts than the small farmers could supply. Ben and Jerry discovered they needed to buy nuts from a large corporation to keep up with the demand for Rainforest Crunch. The big company ended up running the natives out of business. Some sold their land to ranchers and logging companies, and more rainforest was cut down.

Working with Workers

Ben and Jerry ran into other troubles even as they tried to help the poor and powerless. As the demand for their ice cream continued to grow, people who worked at Ben & Jerry's factories often had to work long hours with equipment that broke down. Working conditions were difficult in other ways as well. In summer, boiling kettles made the air in the factory terribly hot. And some workers injured their wrists trying to get the candy rolled out thin enough to pass Ben's taste test for crunchiness.

Although they labored under difficult conditions, the workers at the candy company were given a 10 percent share of the profits, unlike most factory workers.

Ben (left) and Jerry, shown here at a company party in 1990, gave their employees generous benefits, including three pints of ice cream for every full day they worked.

They were also given generous medical benefits and a day care center for their children. And each employee was given three pints of ice cream for every full workday.

Ben and Jerry were so pleased with their new way of running a business that they decided to share it with others. In 1997 they published *Ben & Jerry's Double Dip: Lead with Your Values and Make Money Too*. In the book the men explained what they had learned about trying to bring better social conditions into their business relationships.

The End and Beginning

In 1999 several large corporations that owned other ice cream companies wanted to buy out Ben & Jerry's.

While such a sale would bring Ben and Jerry millions of dollars, people in Vermont were unhappy. Vermont governor Howard Dean said, "This company has come to symbolize Vermont . . . it would really be a shame if it were [sold to a large corporation from out of state]."[5] Despite this attitude, in August 2000 Ben and Jerry sold their ice cream company for $326 million to a large corporation with operations in eighty-eight nations.

Ben (left) and Jerry fed Unilever chief executive officer Richard Goldstein ice cream after Unilever bought Ben & Jerry's for $326 million in 2000.

After the buyout Ben and Jerry continued to make appearances to promote the company they started. They spoke to large groups and promoted environmental causes. They stayed active in Businesses for Social Responsibility, helping to buy companies in low-income communities to raise wages and benefits and improve working conditions.

Jerry helps to direct the Institute for Sustainable Communities, which helps communities all over the world to solve environmental, economic, and social problems. Starting in 2002 Ben helped register voters and educate them about democracy with parades, fairs, and a Web site, www.truemajority.org. He organized the Rolling Thunder Down Home Democracy Tour, a traveling fair that promoted liberal causes and voter registration.

Although they are multimillionaires today, Ben and Jerry worked very hard for years to turn their dream into a world-famous ice cream brand. Through it all they tried to remain true to the ideals they had in college, of a world where equality and justice were important values. Although they did not always succeed, many feel that Ben Cohen and Jerry Greenfield have provided a new model for businesses that want to help make the world a better place to live.

Notes

Chapter One: Two Kids from Long Island
1. Quoted in Fred "Chico" Lager, *Ben & Jerry's: The Inside Scoop.* New York: Crown, 1994, p. 1.

Chapter Two: The Ice Cream Shop
2. Quoted in Gale Research, "Jerry Greenfield," *Business Leader Profiles for Students,* vol. 1, 1999. http://galenet. galegroup.com/servlet/BioRC (Document Number: K1604000097).
3. Quoted in Lager, *Ben & Jerry's,* p. 144.

Chapter Four: Giving Back
4. Quoted in Lager, *Ben & Jerry's,* p. 157.
5. Quoted in Gale Research, "Jerry Greenfield."

Glossary

biochemistry: The study of life processes and chemical substances that occur in living organisms.

cinder block: A hollow building block made with concrete and coal ashes.

conservation: Preserving natural resources, such as forests and water systems, from loss or damage.

corporation: A large company.

debate: To engage in an argument and discuss opposing viewpoints.

distributor: A company that buys products from a manufacturer and delivers them for sale to stores such as supermarkets.

hippie: A person who opposes and rejects many of the traditions, standards, and customs of society.

premed: Classes that prepare a student for medical school.

For Further Exploration

Books

Ben Cohen and Jerry Greenfield with Nancy J. Stevens, *Ben & Jerry's Homemade Ice Cream and Dessert Book*. New York: Workman, 1987. Ben and Jerry share their story, their ice cream theory, and ninety recipes to make at home, including sorbets, giant sundaes, and other ice cream dishes.

Laura French, *Internet Pioneers: The Cyber Elite*. Berkeley Heights, NJ: Enslow, 2001. This book includes ten biographies of pioneers who have helped change the world by thinking differently and making basic changes in the world of business.

William Jaspersohn, *Ice Cream*. New York: Macmillan, 1988. This book takes the reader on a behind-the-scenes tour of Ben & Jerry's ice cream factory in Waterbury, Vermont. It explains where ice cream comes from and how it is made.

Barbara Lewis, *The Kids' Guide to Social Action: How to Solve the Social Problems You Choose—and Turn Creative Thinking into Positive Action*. Minneapolis: Free Spirit, 1998. A book that teaches children political action skills that can help them make a difference by solving social problems at community, state, and national levels.

Diane Mayr, *The Everything Kids' Money Book*. Holbrook, MA: Adams Media, 2000. This book explains the history of money as a medium of exchange, making and spending money, banking, and investing.

Web Sites

Ben and Jerry's (www.central-vt.com/web/benjerry). The thirty-minute Ben & Jerry's ice cream factory tour is Vermont's number-one tourist attraction. This site includes maps and lists of places to visit near the Ben & Jerry's factory in Vermont.

Ben & Jerry's Ice Cream (www.benjerry.com). Ben & Jerry's official Web site includes fun and games, recipes, e-cards, history lessons about the company and the ice cream, a gift shop, and more.

Chunky Monkey Fan Club (www.chunkymonkey.com). This Web site tells the inside story of the real Chunky Monkey behind Ben & Jerry's Chunky Monkey flavor ice cream. The Web site includes many fun art projects such as a cartoon drawing lesson, stories, and poems about Chunky Monkey, and other funny animals.

Index

Picture Credits

Cover image: © CORBIS Sygma
AP/Wide World Photos, 30, 34, 39
© James P. Blair/CORBIS, 18
Classmates.com Yearbook Archives, 9 (both)
© CORBIS Sygma, 16
© Henry Diltz/CORBIS, 36
Kim Grant/Lonely Planet Images, 12
© Jon Hicks/CORBIS, 7
© Bob Krist/CORBIS, 11, 20
Steve Liss/Time Life Pictures/Getty Images, 29, 33, 38
© Richard T. Nowitz/CORBIS, 25, 26
Fred Prouser/Reuters/Landov, 19

About the Author

P.M. Boekhoff is the author of more than twenty-five nonfiction books for children. She has written about history, science, and the lives of creative people. In addition, Boekhoff is an artist who has created murals and theatrical scenic paintings and has illustrated many book covers. In her spare time she paints, draws, writes poetry, and studies herbal medicine.